CYC

BUILDING FAMILY FAITH THROUGH LENT

LISA M. BELLECCI-ST.ROMAIN

LIGUORI
PUBLICATIONS

ONE LIGUORI DRIVE
LIGUORI, MO 63057-9999
(314) 464-2500

Imprimi Potest:
Richard Thibodeau, C.SS.R.
Provincial, Denver Province
The Redemptorists

Imprimatur:
+ Paul A. Zipfel, V.G.
Auxiliary Bishop, Archdiocese of St. Louis

ISBN 0-89243-808-8
Library of Congress Catalog Card Number: 94-79444

Copyright © 1997, Lisa M. Bellecci-st.romain
Printed in the United States of America
01 00 99 98 97   5 4 3 2 1

All rights reserved. No part of this booklet may be reproduced, stored in a retrieval system, or transmitted without the written permission of Liguori Publications.

Cover and interior art by Chris Sharp

Calendar

Page	Sunday or Feast	1997	2000	2003
9	1st Sun. of Lent	16 Feb.	12 Mar.	9 Mar.
12	2nd Sun. of Lent	23 Feb.	—	16 Mar.
14	St. Joseph	—	19 Mar.	—
17	3rd Sun. of Lent	2 Mar.	26 Mar.	23 Mar.
20	4th Sun. of Lent	9 Mar.	2 Apr.	30 Mar.
22	5th Sun. of Lent	16 Mar.	9 Apr.	6 Apr.
24	Passion Sunday	23 Mar.	16 Apr.	13 Apr.
29	Easter Sunday	30 Mar.	23 Apr.	20 Apr.

Introduction

■■■■■■

HAVE YOU WISHED for a book that could help you share your faith with your children, a book that does not bore them or become tedious for you?

This book is that book! It gives your family a chance to share and think, while having fun with one another. As a family, you can study the Sunday Scriptures to make them come alive for your children. (Some weeks cite only a portion of the entire reading.) How you use the questions for reflection depends on the ages of your children or their desire to consider the issues. Use your judgment; see what works each week and what feels complete.

Each session is designed to last about fifteen minutes, but there might be times when a good discussion keeps the session going longer.

Some sessions require additional time and effort on the part of the leader.

All sessions end with a "treat" (suggestions provided). Sugar-free dietary needs have been considered, and many suggestions are available in both sugar and nonsugar forms. If you don't find the treat appropriate, choose something else. Enjoy your treat around the table or in the family meeting place to reinforce a sense of family unity.

The items needed for each session are generally those found around the house; options, however, are provided. The leader has the responsibility of gathering the items for his or her week and making any necessary advance preparations. Note: the leader need not always be a parent in the household. Grandparents or other relatives might like a turn, and older children can benefit from leading something fun, yet Scripture-oriented. The leader, however, should be old enough to take precautions around young children when materials and activities call for safety.

Set aside one special place in your house for your family's altar. It could be a corner table, the top of the television, the middle of the kitchen or dining-room table—anywhere your family decides. Each week the text will suggest placing something on the family altar space for the week. Thus, the space should not inconvenience family routine.

To accommodate family schedules, it's important to set aside a regular time to gather the family. Some families prefer to gather before Sunday liturgy, to have an idea of what's coming up at church. Others gather the following week, to continue what they heard at church on Sunday. You decide what fits your family's schedule and preferences. With weekly regularity, growth and good times are guaranteed!

THE SEASON OF LENT

First Sunday of Lent

Theme: We are not alone.

Reading: *Mark 1:12-15 (Gospel)*
The Spirit sent Jesus out toward the desert. Jesus stayed in the wasteland forty days, put to the test there by Satan. He was with the wild beasts, and angels waited on him.

After John the Baptist's arrest, Jesus appeared in Galilee proclaiming God's good news: "This is the time of fulfillment. The reign of God is at hand! Reform your lives and believe in the good news!"

Materials: ✓ a clear area (free of floor clutter, wall hangings, and so forth to create a look of barrenness) ✓ pictures or newspaper clippings about evil things ✓ pieces of paper ✓ crucifix or cross ✓ one piece of paper with ANGELS written on it (or a drawing of an angeltype figure) ✓ pencil

Treat: animal crackers (wild beasts)

Leader's Instructions: Scatter the newspaper clippings and/or pictures around the floor. Gather the family, and have them sit on the floor (unless their health prohibits it). Open with prayer, read the Scripture, and lead the Share and Commit sections.

Share: Although we don't all go to a desert to be purified and tested, we do sometimes feel both fearful and tested in our everyday lives.

Have you ever felt like you were in a wasteland? (Ask someone to share his or her experience of a wasteland.) Why do we get these feelings? Have you ever felt like "wild beasts" were surrounding you? What happened? (Ask someone to write the responses on the blank papers and scatter them on the floor.)

Do you feel surrounded by evil or skewed values in society? Would you consider these "wild beasts"? What are some examples?

(Bring out the cross or crucifix and the ANGELS.) Fortunately, we are not alone as we feel put to the test in this life. Jesus and the angels are able to help us.

What do you think Jesus would do or would want us to do about the evils we have around us? If we choose to act on any of these, we would be joining Jesus in declaring the reign of God at hand. Does knowing that give you courage to act?

Commit: At least once each week during this season of Lent, let's do something (letterwriting, boycotting, speaking out, aiding those in need or who have been harmed) to join Jesus in declaring the reign of God at hand.

Altar Sign: Place the cross or crucifix and the ANGELS on the altar space as a reminder to follow through on your commitments. Consider leaving one or both of these items there all through Lent to remind persons to follow through on their commitments.

Prayer: God, ever close to us, we thank you for our lives. We pray that we might use them during this season of Lent to bring goodness into the wasteland. We pray for the graces of courage and humility as we go about your work. Amen.

Close: Give one another a hug, enjoy your treats, and help put the room back in order.

Second Sunday of Lent

Theme: God is with us through "thick and thin."

Reading: *Romans 8:31-34 (Reading II)*
If God is for us, who can be against us? Is it possible that God, who did not spare Jesus but handed him over for the sake of us all will not grant us all things besides? Who shall bring a charge against God's chosen ones? God, who justifies? Who shall condemn them? Christ Jesus who died or rather was raised up, who is at the right hand of God and who intercedes for us?

Materials: ✓ a deck of cards, all four aces on top

Treat: crackers and cheese (thin and thick slices)

Leader's Instructions: Gather the family, open with prayer, read the Scripture, and lead the Share and Commit sections.

Share: Sometimes it might be nice if life was like playing cards. If you get four aces (turn them faceup one at a time), you know that no one can argue with that. But in life, it seems like people cheat, betray your friendship, or cast you aside because of what you're doing.

Lent is a good time to pause and get a bigger picture. We can trust in God, no matter what the hardship, because for our sakes, God gave us Jesus.

Are you struggling now with situations of being cheated, betrayed, or left out because of some unpopular stance or action you've taken? What are the feelings you experience? How are you coping with these? Can any of us help you remember the "bigger picture"? How does remembering the "bigger picture" help get us through the bad times?

Do you recall ever cheating, betraying, or leaving others out? Why did you do that? Would you do it again if you had the chance to do it over? How does it feel to know that Christ does not condemn you for those actions, but rather intercedes for you and calls you to holiness?

Commit: This Lent, let's stop any cheating, betraying, or ridiculing we might be doing to others. Let's continue to do God-centered activities, in spite of being left out or ridiculed.

Altar Sign: Place the four aces faceup on the altar space as a sign of the victory you have because God is for you.

Prayer: Merciful God, we trust in your goodness and love because of Jesus. May we always remember that struggle does not mean failure, and death is not the end. We pray for the grace to follow you through "thick and thin." Amen.

Close: Enjoy a game of cards. Share a hug, and enjoy the treat.

Saint Joseph, Husband of Mary

Theme: God asks us to be upright and loving.

Reading: *Matthew 1:16, 18-21, 24 (Gospel)*
Jacob was the father of Joseph the husband of Mary. It is of her that Jesus who is called the Messiah was born. Now this is how the birth of Jesus Christ came about. When his mother Mary was engaged to Joseph, but before they lived together, she was found with child through the power of the Holy Spirit. Joseph her husband, an upright man unwilling to expose her to the law, decided to divorce her quietly. Such was his intention when suddenly the angel of God appeared in a dream and said to him: "Joseph, son of David, have no fear about taking Mary as your wife. It is by the Holy Spirit that she has conceived this child. She is to have a son and you are to name him Jesus because he will save his people from their sins." When Joseph awoke he did as the angel of God had directed him.

Materials: ✓ books (one per person)

Treat: some treat that can be stacked and balanced, such as candy bars or granola bars

Leader's Instructions: Gather the family, and open with prayer. Give one book to each person. Ask each person to take turns walking across the room with the book balanced on his or her head. Read the Scripture, and lead the Share and Commit sections.

Share: How easy was it for you to be "upright" and balance the book on your head?

In addition to being upright, Joseph was asked to be loving. How was he asked to be loving? Why would Joseph be willing to do what he was asked? What do you think Joseph might have been feeling before he had the dream? after he had the dream?

Let's take a few minutes to practice being "upright" and loving. This time, balance the book on your head as you hug someone. (When each person has had an opportunity to try this, continue.)

Was it even harder than just being "upright"? Imagine that God is asking you to be loving toward someone who has offended you. Would you be willing to act lovingly out of your love for God?

How do you know when God is inviting you to go beyond "your rights" and be loving to someone?

Commit: This week, let's listen to God asking us to go beyond "being right" and "upright" to being loving.

Altar Sign: Stack the books on the altar space as a reminder to balance rights and love.

Prayer: Dear God, you love us even when we make mistakes, and you ask us to love others. May we trust in you enough to give up our rights and to act with love toward others who offend us. We pray for the same treatment when we offend others. May we all come closer to the joy of unity with you. Amen.

Close: Take time to practice further the art of being "upright" (balancing the book on your head) and being loving (hugging one another). Enjoy the treat.

Third Sunday of Lent

Theme: Let us be clean, inside and out.

Reading: *John 2:13-25 (Gospel)*
As the Jewish Passover was near, Jesus went up to Jerusalem. In the temple precincts he came upon people engaged in selling oxen, sheep, and doves, and others seated changing coins. Jesus made a kind of whip of cords and drove them all out of the temple area, sheep and oxen alike, and knocked over the moneychangers' tables, spilling their coins. Jesus told those who were selling doves, "Get them out of here! Stop turning my Father's house into a marketplace!" His disciples recalled the words of Scripture, "Zeal for your house consumes me."

At this, the Jews responded, "What sign can you show us authorizing you to do these things?" "Destroy this temple," was Jesus' answer, "and in three days I will raise it up." They retorted, "This temple took forty-six years to build, and you are going to 'raise it up in three days!'" Actually, Jesus was talking about the temple of his body. Only after Jesus had been raised from the dead did his disciples recall that he had said this and come to believe the Scripture and the word he had spoken.

While Jesus was in Jerusalem during the Passover festival, many believed in his name, for they could see the signs he was performing. For his part, Jesus would not trust himself to them, because he knew them all. Jesus needed no one to give him testimony about human nature. He was well aware of what was in the human heart.

Materials: ✓ scrub brushes, sponges, and rags (one per person) ✓ bucket of soapy water ✓ timer or watch with a sweep hand ✓ a blank sheet of paper ✓ pen or pencil

Treat: a refreshing drink (such as a root-beer float or a blender drink)

Leader's Instructions: Choose a wall, cupboard, floor, or room that needs cleaning. Gather the family in that space, and open with prayer. Explain that today, before the reading, the family has a task to do as a preparation: a joint cleaning project that will take five or ten minutes. (Anyone who cannot participate in the cleaning can serve as a supervisor.) Show the family the spot, assign certain areas to certain people depending on their height and abilities, set the timer (or start timing with a watch), and tell the family, "Go!"

■ ■ ■ 16

When time is up, collect the scrubbing materials, and settle into a group for the remainder of your time together. Read the Scripture, and lead the Share and Commit sections.

Share: How is Jesus' cleansing of the Temple the same as, and different from, the cleaning we just did? (Ask someone to list the responses on the sheet of paper.) How are those the same as, and different from, "cleansing" our souls?

Is cleaning more tolerable when done with others? How does this relate to our individual spiritual journeys? How can we journey together as a family?

What do you think was Jesus' motivation in clearing the Temple? What might he think needs clearing in our souls?

Commit: This week, let's share our spiritual struggles with at least one other person in our family.

Altar Sign: Place some of the scrubbing materials on a tray or in a container on the altar space as a reminder to keep working on "cleaning" the negative and fearful from your souls.

Prayer: Dear Jesus, our savior and friend, we thank you for sharing with us the intense love you have for God our creator. May we be so moved to focus our praise and worship on God. We pray for the grace to be spiritually clean. Amen.

Close: Let anyone who feels like scrubbing do some more! Enjoy your treat, and give one another a hug.

Fourth Sunday of Lent

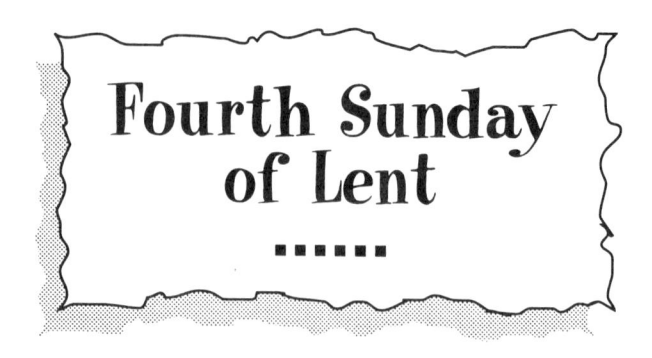

Theme: We are truly God's handiwork.

Reading: *Ephesians 2:4-10 (Reading II)*
God is rich in mercy; because of God's great love for us we were brought to life with Christ when we were dead in sin. By this favor you were saved. Both with and in Christ Jesus, God raised us up and gave us a place in the heavens, that in ages to come God might display the great wealth of such favor, manifested by kindness to us in Christ Jesus. I repeat, it is owing to God's favor that salvation is yours through faith. This is not your own doing, it is God's gift; neither is it a reward for anything you have accomplished, so let no one pride themselves on it. We are truly God's handiwork, created in Christ Jesus to lead the life of good deeds which God prepared for us in advance.

Materials: ✓ examples of human handiwork (embroidery, carpentry, clothing, or painting) ✓ watercolor brushes ✓ watercolors (optional) ✓ paper (optional)

Treat: basic cookie recipe, with three or four colors of icing to decorate them

Leader's Instructions: Gather the family, and place the articles of handiwork in the center of the group. Open with prayer, read the Scripture, and lead the Share and Commit sections.

Share: Does a painting take pride in how it looks? Does an item of carpentry take pride in its beauty? It would be silly, for its purpose was to be used to make something beautiful. Our purpose is the same, as we heard in this reading.

Do you agree that salvation is not your own doing? Why do you agree or disagree? If you can't earn salvation, where do the "good works" come in? Do you ever feel tempted to think you cannot be saved or that you have done all you've accomplished by yourself? What helps you remember the truth about this?

If you could be a perfect piece of handiwork that God made, what would you be? Something sewn? carved? woven? hammered and nailed? painted? shaped? Why do you pick that?

Commit: Each morning this week, let's get out of bed and say to ourselves, "I am God's handiwork!" Let's do whatever good work we feel God is calling us to do. Let's teach a craft we know to someone who wants to learn it.

Altar Sign: Place the various objects of handiwork on the altar space or near it as a reminder of the beauty in each person: God's very special handiwork!

Prayer: God of creation, God of glory, your design for the universe and for our very lives is only for glory. We want to be willing partners in your design. We pray for the grace of humility where good works are involved; we pray for the grace to trust you when we are tempted to hold back. Amen.

Close: Using the watercolor brushes, decorate the cookies with icing. Enjoy your treat, and give everyone a hug. Use the watercolors, paper, and brushes to create some handiwork together.

Fifth Sunday of Lent

Theme: God writes upon our hearts.

Reading: *Jeremiah 31:31-34 (Reading I)*
The days are coming, says our God, when I will make a new covenant with the house of Israel and the house of Judah. It will not be like the covenant I made with their ancestors the day I took them by the hand to lead them forth from the land of Egypt; for they broke my covenant, and I had to show myself their master, says our God.

But this is the covenant which I will make with the house of Israel after those days, says our God. I will place my law within them, and write it upon their hearts; I will be their God, and they shall be my people. No longer will they have need to teach their friends and kin how to know God. All, from least to greatest, shall know me, says our God, for I will forgive their evildoing and remember their sins no more.

Materials: ✓ Play-Doh™ or modeling clay (enough for each person to make a heart) ✓ a heart-shaped cookie cutter or some blunt knives ✓ pencils

Treat: cinnamon toast (Use the heart-shaped cookie cutter to make these into hearts too!)

Leader's Instructions: Gather the family, open with prayer, read the Scripture, and lead the Share and Commit sections.

Share: God doesn't give up on people! That's what this reading tells us. God made a "deal," a covenant, with the Hebrews when Moses was told to lead them from Egypt, but they broke their side of the deal. About six hundred years later, this prophet named Jeremiah tells people that God wants to try a covenant again—but this time, God will write the love and law of the covenant within people so they won't forget their part of the agreement.

How did you come to know God's law? If you learned it in your head, do you think it is automatically written on your heart? How does conscience relate to God's law? How can a person's conscience be dulled? Do you think that the movies and TV shows you watch make your conscience dull or sharper? How?

Do you think God is foolish to keep on trying to reach us? What do you usually do when people break their promises with you? Do you keep the promises you make to others?

What word or words best describe how you feel about God wanting to make a covenant with you? Write that on your clay heart.

Commit: This week, let's thank God every day for continually reaching out to us. Let's listen for God's word in our hearts.

Altar Sign: Place the family's decorated hearts on the altar space as a celebration of God's desire to be in covenant with you as individuals and as a family.

Prayer: Loving God, you never let go of us. We ask forgiveness for the times we have turned from you in anger, frustration, confusion, and disappointment. We pray for the grace to be faithful to you no matter what happens in our earthly lives. Amen.

Close: Share a hug with one another, and enjoy your treats.

Passion Sunday
(PALM SUNDAY)

Theme: We want to have an attitude of obedience to God.

Reading: *Philippians 2:6-11 (Reading II)*
Your attitude must be Christ's: though he was in the form of God, he did not deem equality with God something to be grasped at. Rather, he emptied himself, and took the form of a slave, being born in the likeness of humans. He was known to be of human estate, and it was thus that he humbled himself, obediently accepting even death, death on a cross! Because of this, God highly exalted him and bestowed on him the name above every other name, so that at Jesus' name every knee must bend in the heavens, on the earth, and under the earth, and every tongue proclaim to the glory of God the creator: Jesus Christ is Lord!

Materials: ✓ an empty container that held a special treat (ice cream, chocolates, and so forth) ✓ rocks of various sizes that will fit into the container ✓ rock-shaped pieces of paper ✓ pencils (one per person)

Treat: chips, small crackers, or hard pieces of candy that are laid out in the shape of letters to spell the name J-E-S-U-S

Leader's Instructions: Gather the family, and put the empty container in the middle of the circle. Open with prayer, and explain that *obedience* is not a very popular word in the world. People like to think of themselves as independent; they do what they want. Yet, there are many ways people are asked to be obedient every day, such as obeying traffic signals, paying sales taxes, and refraining from violence. Point out to the family that Scripture adds another aspect to the concept of obedience.

Read the Scripture, dropping the rocks in the container as you read "took the form of a slave" and finish dropping them as you read "death on a cross!" Lead the Share and Commit sections.

Share: Who are some of the people and laws you are asked to obey daily? Are any of these a struggle for you?

Why are you asked to be obedient? Are you obeying God when you obey other laws?

Where or when do you feel tempted to disobey? How might we help you with these temptations?

Do you think there can be obedience *and* negotiation in a problem situation in our family? Are you satisfied with how our family negotiates? Are you satisfied with how most of us obey when it is called for?

Adults, what do you remember about having to obey and being able to talk about a problem when you were growing up?

(Have persons write on the rock-shaped pieces of paper a word or two about their struggles with obedience. Place these in the container with the rocks.)

Are there any laws you believe are unjust? Are there times when it seems worth the consequences to disobey certain laws? How does it compare with the kinds of religious laws that Jesus disobeyed? Why, do you think, did Jesus disobey those religious laws?

Commit: This week, let's be obedient in the ways God is calling us in relationships, at work, at school, or within ourselves.

Altar Sign: Place the container of rocks on the altar space as a sign of joining your struggles with the sufferings of Christ.

Prayer: (Raise the container over your head as you pray.) God of mercy and love, we thank you for the faithfulness of your Son, Jesus, whose obedience gained so much for us. We pray for the grace to be obedient in our daily lives, as we hear you asking us. We pray for wisdom to deal with those laws which we believe are unjust, as we hear you leading us. Amen.

Close: Give one another a hug. Share your treat, praying to "absorb" an attitude like Jesus.'

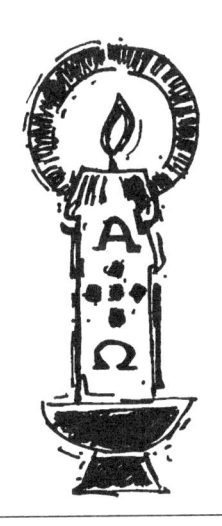

THE SEASON OF EASTER

Easter Sunday

Theme: We can start over.

Reading: *1 Corinthians 5:6-8 (Reading II)*
Do you not know that a little yeast has its effect all through the dough? Get rid of the old yeast to make yourselves fresh dough, unleavened loaves, as it were; Christ, our Passover, has been sacrificed. Let us celebrate the feast not with the old yeast, that of corruption and wickedness, but with the unleavened bread of sincerity and truth.

Materials: ✓ a candle ✓ two pieces of paper ✓ red and green crayons or markers

Treat: a sweet bread

Leader's Instructions: If you choose to make the sweetbread dough, consider having family members help you put it together and/or shape their initials. Then, while the bread is baking, the family can go on with the session.

Before gathering the family, print the word CORRUPTION on one of the pieces of paper. Print SINCERITY on the other piece of paper.

Gather the family, light the candle, and open with prayer. Explain to the family that the reading they are going to hear is about starting over completely free from anything that tempts us to be bad or wicked: the "old yeast."

Read the Scripture, and lead the Share and Commit sections.

Share: What are some wrong or bad things we might do? (Ask someone to use the red marker to write on the CORRUPTION paper one bad thing that begins with each letter of the word. For example, "Cheat," for the "C"; "Omit the truth" for the "O," and so forth.)

What are some good or helpful things we might do? (Ask someone to use the green marker to write on the SINCERITY paper one good thing that begins with each letter of the word. "Standing up for what is right" for the "S"; "Inviting a lonely person to come for a meal" for the "I,". and so forth.)

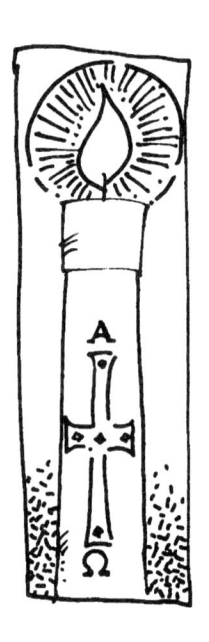

Do you think really being sincere and good is possible here on earth? Why or why not? How can we help one another be more sincere and good?

Commit: Each day this week, let's do one thing we listed on the SINCERITY paper. Let's resist doing the things on the CORRUPTION paper.

Altar Sign: Extinguish the candle, and place it on the altar space as a sign of your joy in the victory of Christ. For this week, tape the two word lists on the wall near the altar space to remind everyone to increase in sincerity and decrease in corruption.

Prayer: God of all goodness and life, today we celebrate the Resurrection of Jesus Christ. We pray for the transformation that will allow us to join you in life everlasting. May our actions shape our hearts and minds and bring us closer to you. Amen.

Close: Eat your bread initials as they are or spread them with icing. Give one another a hug, and have a joyful week!

Also available...

Building Family Faith Through Lent
Cycles A & C
$2.95 each

Building Family Faith
Weekly Lectionary-Based Activities
Cycles A, B, & C
by Lisa Bellecci-st.romain

Includes weekly sharing and study sessions for each Church season (Advent, Christmas, Ordinary Time, Lent, and Easter). **$10.95 each**

More Lenten resources for the family from Liguori...

Lent Begins at Home
Family Prayers and Activities
by Pat and Rosemary Ryan

Help your whole family share the true meaning of Lent through Bible readings, collages, charitable acts, prayers, recipes, and more. **$3.95**

Lent Is for Children
Stories, Activities, Prayers
Revised and Expanded
by Julie Keleman

Imaginative ways to introduce children to Lenten basics such as fasting, temptation, and reconciliation. Now revised with new games and activities, children will discover not just the "how to" of Lenten practices, but the "why" behind them. **$3.95**

Order from your local bookstore or write
Liguori Publications
Box 060, Liguori, MO 63057-9999

Please add 15% of total ($3.50 minimum, $15 maximum) for shipping and handling. For faster service on orders over $20 call toll free 1-800-325-9521, Dept. 060. Please have your credit card handy.